HR Approved Way To Say Things I Can't Say Out Loud At Work

Published by Upgraded Books

More From Upgraded Books

- *HR Approved Ways To Say Things I Can't Say Out Loud At Work*
- *Ways To Make Your Coworkers Feel Awkward*
- *52 Ways to Inform Coworkers They're Stupid*
- *HR Approved Ways To Look Smart At Work*
- *Brilliant Ideas I Had While Taking A Dump*
- *HR Unapproved Ways To Be A Low Impact Hire*
- *Things I Want To Say That Would Get Me Fired*

This book has been approved by Human Resources

Disclaimer: Well, not really!

Download Your Free Guide

Email Like A Pro Cheat Sheet: *HR Approved Ways of Emailing Your Annoying Coworkers*

https://bit.ly/465COao

Note From HR

To Our Hardworking Employee,

We here at Human Resources care very deeply about your mental well-being (and, let's be honest, we'd also like to avoid a high turnover rate, if possible). I know that working here comes with its fair share of challenges, so as a small gesture of support, we're giving you this book to help during those inevitable moments when you feel like you just need to let off some steam.

Think of this book as a safe space for the things you really want to say (scream?) — but probably shouldn't. Inside, you'll find HR-approved alternatives that will enable you to keep your job (hopefully), project a look of professionalism, and avoid any awkward meetings with us — even though we love seeing you! Well, after a coffee or two... and depending on our mood that day.

Enjoy, laugh, and turn to these pages as often as needed to stay somewhat sane.

Happy reading,
Karen from HR

P.S. Keep an eye out for the occasional Case Files I've sprinkled in — they'll show you how these "translations" can be put to use in the wild.

What You Really Want To Say:

No, you fuckwit

HR Approved Alternative:

Let me check with my team and get back to you

Case File

It's Friday — 4:57 p.m. You've already mentally clocked out.

Your bag is packed, your coat is on the back of your chair, and the only thing standing between you and a well-earned weekend is clicking *Shut Down* on your laptop.

That's when your email dings.

Oh no.

You glance at the sender. It's Jax from upper management. The man has never responded to an email on time *in his life,* and yet somehow, he has chosen this exact moment — three minutes before the weekend — to ruin yours.

You hesitate. Maybe if you don't open it, it doesn't exist.

The notification pops up again, though.

Yup, Jax:

"Hey, any chance you can whip up a quick market trend analysis for Monday's leadership meeting? Shouldn't take long — just need a few slides with some key insights. Thanks!"

Shouldn't take long? This is a 30-page data report on a project you weren't even involved in. Jax, of course, was involved but spent every meeting nodding and adding "Just throwing this out there..." before saying something completely useless.

You stare at the email, rage bubbling inside you.

Your fingers hover over the keyboard, tempted to type:

NO, YOU FUCKWIT!

You may even want to throw in: *Do I look like a PowerPoint fairy who can conjure up data analysis out of thin air? It is Friday, Jax! GO HOME.*

But you like having a job, and so, you breathe in... breathe out... and type:

"Let me check with my team and get back to you."

In your head? *I will absolutely not be checking with my team. My team is already at happy hour. My team is three margaritas deep. My team does not exist right now.*

Jax replies immediately:

“Oh great, really appreciate it! Have a good weekend!”

You stare at the screen.

Oh, I will have a good weekend. Because I am not doing this presentation until Monday morning at exactly 8:59 a.m.

You shut your laptop.

The margaritas are calling.

What You Really Want To Say:

Let's get this shit out in the open

HR Approved Alternative:

In the interest of transparency

It's Monday morning, and you're sitting in yet another very important meeting that could have 100% been an email. The topic? Why the new inventory system rollout is behind schedule.

The reason? Oh, everyone in the room already knows, but no one is willing to say it out loud.

Your project manager, Karen (who somehow got this leadership position despite never actually leading anything), clears her throat and begins:

"So, team... does anyone have any insights on why we're experiencing these delays?"

There's silence and awkward eye contact, but nobody responds.

You look around. Oh, we *all* know why.

Maybe it's because the project was assigned to Dave, whose work ethic is as questionable as his browser history. Maybe it's because upper management has changed the project scope five times in the last two weeks. Or maybe—just maybe—it's because Karen herself spent three weeks "workshopping" a decision that should have taken five minutes.

Your patience is running thin. Every bone in your body wants to slam your hands on the table and yell:

"Let's get this shit out in the open!"

But corporate etiquette demands something... softer. So, instead, you plaster on your best I-totally-care-about-this face and say:

"In the interest of transparency, I think it would be helpful to address some of the recurring challenges we've been facing."

What You Really Want To Say:

I have no fucking idea what I'm talking about

HR Approved Alternative:

Let's take a 30,000 foot view here

Case File

You're in a meeting that you definitely should have prepared for.

Maybe it's because the invite was sent at 10 p.m. last night with zero context.

Maybe it's because the topic has changed three times, and nobody knows what's actually being discussed.

Or maybe — just maybe — it's because you simply do not care.

Either way, you're sitting there, nodding along like you understand, hoping no one asks you a direct question.

Then it happens.

Your supervisor, Linda, turns to you and asks:

"So, Ruth, what are your thoughts on leveraging scalable solutions?"

Your soul leaves your body.

Linda might as well have asked you to explain quantum physics in Swahili.

You could have weeks to prepare and still not know what the hell is going on.

But right now? Right now, you have nothing.

No clue. No strategy. No plan.

Just pure, unfiltered panic.

You begin jibber-jabbering, knowing very well you're talking nonsense, and half the people in the room know that too.

Then Melissa, wanting to call you out on your lie, puts you on the spot:

"That's interesting. Can you elaborate more on the last part?"

You briefly consider being honest and saying:

“I have no fucking idea what I’m talking about.”

But you also enjoy things like, say, purchasing groceries for your family and being able to pay rent.

So instead, you inhale, clasp your hands together like you totally have this under control, and say:

“Let’s take a 30,000-foot view here and really consider the implications of leveraging scalable solutions. I can circle back after looping in key stakeholders.”

Your supervisor and everyone else in the meeting nod thoughtfully, and you mentally give yourself a pat on the shoulder.

You'll live to fight another day.

This page has been intentionally left blank*

*Because HR is still at brunch

What You Want To Say:

Fuck off, idiot

HR Approved Alternative:

With all due respect

It's a regular Tuesday afternoon, and you're just trying to mind your own business — maybe catch up on emails, maybe pretend to work while scrolling on your phone.

Keep life peaceful, you know?

Then, out of nowhere, a notification pops up on your screen.

It's Chad from Marketing.

Chad, whose job seems to involve doing absolutely nothing until the last minute and then somehow making everything your problem.

Here's what he has to say:

Heyyy, quick thing!

Can you whip up a quick graphics revamp for the whole social media campaign? The client sent over new brand guidelines two weeks ago, and I totally forgot to tell you. My bad! But I already told them we'd have the updated designs by the end of the day, so we'd better meet that deadline.

Thanks!

You blink.

Two weeks ago?

The campaign you spent *hours* perfecting?

The one that Chad was supposed to review, but instead spent that time passionately debating whether a hot dog is a sandwich?

You check the time. It's 4:45 p.m.

Your hand twitches.

You're filled with the sudden urge to type:

"Fuck off, idiot!" Perhaps peppered with, "And take your useless marketing skills with you!"

But unfortunately, HR has this weird “no verbally assaulting coworkers” policy.

So instead, you inhale slowly, exhale even slower, and type:

"With all due respect, Chad, this is the first I’ve heard of this request. Given the timeframe, I may not be able to accommodate."

Which, of course, translates to: *You have had these new brand guidelines for two weeks, Chad. TWO WEEKS! And instead of telling me at a normal, reasonable time like a competent adult, you sat on them until the absolute last second and are now making it my problem. I will now be ignoring you until further notice.*

Chad, being Chad, completely misses the passive aggression and replies:

"Oh, you’re the best! Appreciate you!"

You stare at the screen.

A deep, dark rage stirs within you, and you close your laptop, thinking about how much you need a drink.

This blank page is designed to empower stakeholders through reflective whitespace immersion.

What You Really Want To Say:

Stop annoying the shit out of me all the time

HR Approved Alternative:

I'll keep you in the loop

Case File

It's midday, and you're finally in the zone. Your inbox is (somewhat) under control, you've cleared a few tasks, and for the first time all day, you feel mildly productive. You're thinking that maybe—just maybe—you will get through the afternoon without interruption.

Then, Lisa from Accounting pings you:
"Hey, just checking in on the updated budget projections!"

You glance at the time. It has been 45 minutes since she last asked. And no, the answer has not changed since then.

So, you do the mature thing, which is ignoring her.

Five minutes pass, and... it's Lisa: "Hey, just circling back on this!"

You rub your temples. Circling back? Lisa has nothing to circle back *to*. The circle never even took shape because the finance team hasn't sent you the numbers yet!

You take a deep breath, thinking that if you don't respond, she'll take the hint.

But three minutes later? Lisa.

"Not sure if my last message went through! Just following up!"

Your eye twitches and your jaw clenches. You now understand why some people quit their jobs to live in the woods.

What you want to say? "STOP ANNOYING THE SHIT OUT OF ME ALL THE TIME."

As an add-on?

"Lisa, if I had the numbers, you would know. Because I would have sent them. In an email. With a spreadsheet. And a subject line that says 'UPDATED BUDGET PROJECTIONS.'"

But instead, you just type: "I'll keep you in the loop."

And Lisa, completely missing the hint, immediately replies:
"Great, thanks!! Let me know if you hear anything!"

You sit there thinking, *Idiot*! But hey, at least you bought yourself some time!

What You Really Want To Say:

Time to make this idiot-proof because you keep screwing up

HR Approved Alternative:

We’re going to streamline things

It's been weeks. Weeks of trying to fix the same mistake over and over again.

You've explained it in meetings, you've sent step-by-step emails, and for some reason, you even made a quick tutorial video because you thought, *Hey, maybe seeing it in action will help*.

But here you are, once again.

Kyle from Marketing is back.

And, surprise, surprise: he's managed to screw up the same thing for the umpteenth time.

This is Kyle, after all, the guy who has somehow turned a simple three-step process into an ongoing corporate disaster. Kyle, who finds new ways to mess up the same task every single time.

Today? It's about submitting reports. *Again*.

Kyle: Hey! I think the system isn't working.

You already know where this is going, but like a responsible adult, you ask anyway.

Maybe, just maybe, this time, Kyle would have it figured out.

You: What's the issue?

Kyle: It won't let me submit my report.

You take a deep breath, mentally prepare for the worst, and type back: Did you follow the steps I sent?

Kyle: Yep!

You: All of them?

There's silence on the other end. And then...

Kyle: Uh... most of them?

You close your eyes and count to 10, reminding yourself that being independently broke isn't as glamorous as it sounds. Then, you open the file he uploaded. And, of course, it's an absolute train wreck.

The report is missing entire sections, the formatting looks like it was done by a toddler, and for some unknown reason, there's a random photo of a dog in the middle of a chart.

That's likely the reason why the system is rejecting Kyle's upload.

You stare at the screen. *Is Kyle okay? Is he secretly a performance artist, and this is some kind of elaborate prank to make me question all my life choices?*

Your fingers itch to type:

Time to make this idiot-proof because you keep screwing up.

But you know better.

So instead, you take a few seconds to calm down, and type:

"Okay, we're going to streamline things a bit so that the process is simpler and easier to follow. This way, everyone knows exactly what to do, and we can avoid mistakes."

The final nail in the coffin comes with Kyle's reply:

"Awesome! Looking forward to it!"

You close your laptop.

It's too early for a drink, but hey, it's not too early to start reconsidering every decision that led you to this point!

This Empty Space has been Approved by HR.

All suggestions were deemed inappropriate.

What You Really Want To Say:

Not now. Leave me alone

HR Approved Alternative:

Let’s park this for the moment

You are drowning in work.

Your inbox is a nightmare, your to-do list is longer than a CVS receipt, and you're one small inconvenience away from a full-blown meltdown.

Why? Because you have a deadline in two hours.

Your fingers are flying across the keyboard, your brain is locked in deep focus, and for once, you actually feel like you're making progress.

And then?

Stephanie happens.

Stephanie, from the "I Have No Sense of Timing" Department.

Stephanie, who has a sixth sense for interrupting you at the worst possible moment.

Stephanie, who seems to believe that if she doesn't ask you this very question right this very second, the entire company might collapse.

She materializes next to your desk like some kind of corporate ghost, her face beaming with an idea that definitely could have waited.

"Hey! Got a sec?"

No, you don't got a sec.

You don't even have *half* a sec.

But Stephanie has already pulled up a chair, making herself at home.

She continues, “So, I was thinking about that client satisfaction survey we discussed three weeks ago...”

Ah, yes. The client satisfaction survey.

The survey that isn’t due for another month.

The survey that was already finalized and sent to leadership for approval.

The survey that Stephanie suddenly wants to “rework” because she’s just now decided that maybe the color scheme should be “more inviting.”

Meanwhile, the email you *actually* need to send is sitting there, half-written, screaming for your attention.

You want to say, "Not now. Leave me alone."

Instead, you force a smile so hard it hurts and say:

“Let’s park this for the moment and revisit once I have a bit more bandwidth to give it the attention it deserves.”

You bite your tongue when Stephanie, completely oblivious, nods enthusiastically and adds:

“Oh, yeah, for sure! I’ll check in again later today.”

You watch as she walks away, already plotting your next escape route, knowing full well that this isn’t over.

Blank page strategically deployed to proactively amplify organizational bandwidth, accelerate holistic throughput, and elevate integrated operational synergies.

What You Really Want To Say:

Did you hear a word I just said?

HR Approved Alternative:

Can you clarify your understanding of what we just discussed?

Case File

It's been a long meeting. Like, so long that your coffee has gone cold, your foot has fallen asleep, and you're starting to wonder if time even exists anymore. You have just spent a solid 10 minutes explaining something that should have taken 30 seconds—not because you're bad at explaining, but because you had to repeat yourself three times in three different ways. First, you checked for understanding. Then, you asked if everyone was clear. And on top of that, you even threw in a relatable example, just in case! Anyway, you were feeling pretty good about it. Until...

Greg.

Greg, who has been nodding enthusiastically the whole time. The very same Greg who has been making serious "I totally get it" faces while you were speaking. And yet, the raised hand in the room belongs to him, paired with the eloquent question:

"Wait... so what exactly are we supposed to do?"

The room goes completely silent. You blink. Once. Twice. You stare at Greg, wondering if there's a secret camera recording somewhere, and you're all on the set of *Trigger Happy TV*.

You want to say, "Did you hear a single word I just said?" Or, even better, "Greg, my friend, my guy, my dude... were you even *HERE* just now? Physically? Mentally? *Spiritually*?"

But that would be frowned upon, so instead, you keep your voice even, put on your best "patient professional" face, and say:

"Okay Greg, before I answer that, can you clarify your understanding of what we just discussed?"

You give him the side eye that literally screams, *I am giving you one last chance to prove that you were, in fact, present in this meeting and not mentally on a beach somewhere!*, hoping he'll get the memo. Instead, Greg, still looking confused, squints at the whiteboard, then at his notes, then finally at you, and says:

"Uhh... yeah, so... you want us to... do the thing?"

You exhale slowly. Everyone else avoids eye contact because they, too, have lost the will to live. But you? You are a professional. You nod, put on a smile that doesn't quite reach your eyes, and say: "Yes, Greg. Do the thing."

What You Really Want To Say:

Over my dead body, asshole

HR Approved Alternative:

It's on my roadmap

Case File

It's Monday morning, you've just arrived at the office and have barely had time to take off your coat when an email notification pops up on your screen.

The subject line: *Quick favor!*

You already know. Nothing good ever follows a "quick favor." With a deep sigh, you open the email, and — yep. It's worse than expected.

It's from Olivia in the Procurement department.

Olivia, who somehow has energy before 8 a.m.

Olivia, who has never met a task she couldn't delegate.

Olivia, who uses "team effort" when she means "*your* effort."

Hey there! Hope you had a relaxing weekend! (You didn't.)

Just a quick one: Can you take the lead on cleaning up the supplier contract database? It's a bit messy. Just needs a quick reorganization!

It shouldn't take too long — basically just reviewing 500+ contracts, updating expiration dates, flagging duplicate vendors, and making a master spreadsheet with key terms like payment schedules, penalty clauses, and renewal conditions.

Easy, right? No rush, but I would love to have it done by Friday! Thanks a ton!!!

You stare at the screen, then you do a slow reread.

Olivia has just casually asked you to sort through a whole labyrinth of outdated contracts, many of which were probably written in 2007 by someone who no longer works here.

And she somehow thinks it's a quick task.

Your first instinct?

To type: *Over my dead body, a*$h*le!*

But alas, you have bills to pay. And so, you simply type:

"It’s on my road map."

Hopefully, Olivia will get the message.

Hopefully, she'll even understand that you have absolutely no intention of doing this anytime soon, or maybe ever.

Does she, though? Really?

Of course not! Because two minutes later, she writes you back:

"Omg, you’re the best! I have a *feeling* this is going to be amazing!!"

You sit back and start mentally calculating how much it would cost to quit your job and open a beachside smoothie stand.

Strategic Whitespace.

We’re currently benchmarking the ROI of doing nothing.

What You Really Want To Say:

Don't try me again

HR Approved Alternative:

Going forward

What You Really Want To Say:

No one gives a damn what you think

HR Approved Alternative:

I truly appreciate your input

What You Really Want To Say:

It's time to get over yourself

HR Approved Alternative:

We need to encourage a culture of teamwork

Case File

You're in a team brainstorming session, but at this point, it feels less like a group discussion and more like *The Jessica Show*. Why?

Because Jessica, one of your coworkers, has been talking nonstop for most of the meeting.

She's not just sharing ideas — she's taking over the entire conversation.

Every time someone else tries to speak, she cuts them off with "Yes, but what if we..." or "Actually, I think..."

You glance around the room. Everyone else looks exhausted.

Dave is trying to make it seem like he's listening, and you can tell that Priya — also part of the session — checked out 20 minutes ago.

Even your manager looks like he regrets setting up this meeting.

The worst part? Jessica's "brilliant" ideas are either repeats of old failures or make absolutely no sense at all.

At one point, she suggests something that would actually cost the company money instead of making it.

You're slowly beginning to lose patience, and you have half a mind to stand up and say:

"Jessica, it's time to get over yourself. We get it. You love the sound of your own voice. But the rest of us would like a chance to contribute before we all retire."

But then, that might come off as rude. And HR loves those "be nice to your coworkers" workshops.

So, instead, you raise your hand and say, "We need to encourage a culture of teamwork here. Let's make sure everyone has a chance to share their ideas."

But you know that what you actually mean is:

Jessica, for the love of all that is holy, shut up, and let someone else talk.

The room goes silent.

Jessica looks surprised — maybe even a little offended.

But, miracle of miracles, she actually stops talking.

Dave mouths "Thank you" from across the table.

Priya sits up, ready to finally contribute.

Your manager sighs in relief.

And for the first time all morning, the meeting continues like a normal discussion, with actual teamwork.

As you leave the room, you silently pat yourself on the back.

You have restored balance to the workplace.

If that's not worthy of an award, what is?

This Space is Reserved for an Inspirational Quote.

Don't expect inspiration to strike anytime soon.

What You Really Want To Say:

I'm not going to say this again, you dimwit

HR Approved Alternative:

To reiterate.

It's 3:00 p.m. on a Wednesday, and you're sitting in your fifth Zoom meeting of the day. You are exhausted. Your brain has left the building, and the only thing keeping you going is the thought of your 3:30 p.m. break.

But then, Kevin from Accounting says, "Wait, so just to clarify—are we using the new expense forms or the old ones?"

You stop breathing. Kevin has asked this three times already this week. You sent a company-wide email about this on Monday. You attached a PDF. You even made it dummy-proof with giant red arrows pointing to the new forms. You used a GIF, for crying out loud—a GIF of a dancing monkey holding a sign that literally read, *USE THE NEW FORMS*. You also personally reminded Kevin *yesterday* when he asked the exact same thing.

You look around at your coworkers in their little boxes on Zoom. Some are staring at their screens like they're watching a slow-motion car crash. One person has muted themselves, probably screaming into their hands.

You feel like shouting:

"Kevin, I am not going to say this again, you dimwit! The answer is in your inbox, your trash folder, and probably written on the office bathroom walls at this point!"

But, because you enjoy getting paid, you take a deep breath and say:

"To reiterate, we're using the new expense forms. I've included the link in the chat again for easy reference."

There is a long pause as everyone waits, probably wondering if Kevin finally... understands? Or, they must just be wondering if you're about to lose it on camera.

Then, after what feels like a lifetime, Kevin says: "Ohhh, got it! Thanks for clarifying!"

Do you believe him? Absolutely not. But for the sake of your sanity, you move on, knowing very well that Kevin will be asking the same thing next week.

What You Really Want To Say:

I'm not doing your job for you, you lazy bum

HR Approved Alternative:

That falls outside of my scope.

Case File

It's just minutes to the weekend, and you're mentally already at happy hour—sunglasses on, margarita soon to be in hand, zero f*%ks left to give. Then, like a villain in a bad rom-com, Mia slides into your DMs with the most predictable message of all time:

"Hey! Can you pull that inventory report for me? I need it for my presentation on Monday."

You ball your hands into fists. This is the same report you've shown Mia how to pull three times this quarter. You even made her a step-by-step guide with screenshots, which she immediately archived and never looked at again.

You feel like furiously typing back: *Mia, I'm not doing your job for you, you lazy bum! You know where the data is. You know how to export it. Stop pretending you don't just because you'd rather scroll through funny memes than do actual work!*

However, there's a fat chance Mia might forward your reply to management, leading you to kiss your paycheck goodbye. So, you mentally count to 10 and type back:

"That falls outside of my scope, but I'd be happy to forward you the training guide again."

Her reply is instant:

"Gotcha."

However, you aren't sold because you know what she means is: *I'll wait until 5:00 p.m. on Sunday and then panic-email you.*

You forward her the guide again, tag it with "For your record," and immediately set your status to "Offline" before she can ask you to also "just format it real quick."

What You Really Want To Say:

Listen here, you idiot

HR Approved Alternative:

For future reference

Case File

It's an early morning at the office, and you're already regretting checking your email.

Right at the top of your inbox is a panicked message from Tyler:

"URGENT: System is DOWN! HELP!!!"

You sit up straight. *Is this real? Did the entire system actually crash? Is this the day everything finally falls apart?* You scramble to check the system status. Everything is fine. No errors. No outages. The system is perfectly functional.

So, what's the problem? You take a deep breath and reply:

"Hey, Tyler, what exactly isn't working?"

Five minutes later, he responds:

"Oh! I couldn't log in. But I restarted my computer and now it's fine. Thanks!"

Oh. Oh no. Did Tyler just send a company-wide emergency email because he forgot to restart his laptop?

You clench your fists and consider standing up, marching to Tyler's desk, and saying:

"Listen here, you idiot! The system was never down! Next time, try turning it off and on before declaring a state of emergency!"

But because Tyler would probably report you for "verbal assault," you stick to simply typing:

"For future reference, should you encounter any issues, we recommend performing a system restart as an initial troubleshooting step. If the issue persists, please don't hesitate to reach out."

What You Really Want To Say:

You're just a complete waste of space

HR Approved Alternative:

There's room for improvement

It's performance review season, and you've been dreading this moment for weeks.

You're sitting across from Hailey, the intern who somehow turned "doing absolutely nothing" into an art form.

For most of the past three months, Hailey has accidentally had her out-of-office reply activated when she was *definitely* in the office.

On top of that, she asked you how to attach a file to an email about seven times, and spent 90% of her "workday" loudly chewing gum and watching TikTok compilations at her desk.

Now, as you stare at her "self-evaluation" (which consists of two bullet points and a smiley face), you realize you have to give her feedback. You feel like ripping the Band-Aid and straight up saying:

"Hailey, you're just a complete waste of space. The office plants contribute more than you do, and they're fake. I'm pretty sure the coffee machine has better problem-solving skills."

But then you remind yourself that corporate life requires restraint. You take a moment, look her in the eyes, and say:

"Hailey, your work shows... enthusiasm. That said, there's definitely room for improvement in areas like time management and technical skills. Maybe we could explore some... additional training opportunities?"

Hailey nods enthusiastically. "Yeah, I've been meaning to learn more! Maybe like... a webinar or something?"

You resist the urge to scream.

Instead, you sign her up for the most boring compliance training you can find and make a mental note to hide all the office snacks.

What You Really Want To Say:

Which one of you dumb fucks created this shit show?

HR Approved Alternative:

Can we identify the responsible party?

You walk into the office on Monday morning to discover that someone has completely nuked the shared project database.

What was once a carefully organized spreadsheet to track client relationships and partnership details now contains a full recipe for banana bread (with commentary), 37 cat memes embedded in the comments, and one cell that just says, "*TEST: DO NOT DELETE*" in Comic Sans 72pt font.

The worst part?

This was the master file for tracking key partnership details, including valuable data on corporate sponsorships worth millions in revenue for the next quarter. Your eye starts twitching like a malfunctioning robot, and you just want to ask:

"Which one of you dumb f*%ks created this shit show?"

But you remember that you don't want to be the subject of a future HR training. So, clutching your cup of tea like a stress ball, you politely say:

"Team, can we kindly identify the responsible party here? We need to understand how our sponsorship tracking system became both a cookbook and a meme museum."

After an awkward silence, the new marketing assistant, Beth, timidly raises her hand:

"Um... I think that might have been me. I was trying to make it more... engaging?"

Engaging?

You resist the urge to laugh out loud or cry. Instead, you keep a straight face. Meanwhile, the rest of the team is visibly crumbling, their stifled laughter making them look like they're suffering from some kind of gastrointestinal distress.

You nod slowly and assign her to some data entry training that is so thorough it could prepare her for decoding the Rosetta Stone.

You're leaving nothing to chance here.

What You Really Want To Say:

I'm not dealing with this crap

HR Approved Alternative:

Let me circle back to you

What You Really Want To Say:

Are you fucking kidding me?

HR Approved Alternative:

We strive to go above and beyond

What You Really Want To Say:

Did I ask for your input? No, I didn't, you prick

HR Approved Alternative:

I'll keep that in mind

Case File

You've had a long day, and you're finally putting the finishing touches on the inventory restock proposal—a spreadsheet that's taken two weeks, 20 pivot tables, and more caffeine than your doctor would legally approve. You've triple-checked everything: supplier codes, shipping schedules, everything!

You're proud of your work, and you're ready to hit "Send" and reward yourself with a bag of pretzels and 15 minutes of pretending to "collaborate" in the break room.

But Ethan decides at that moment to walk by. He leans in over your desk, squints at your screen, and says:

"Oh... you're still using that supplier for the restock? Hmm. Bold choice."

You blink. *Bold choice? BOLD CHOICE?!* Ethan's job is balancing invoices, not overseeing warehouse logistics. He once tried to "audit" the snack budget and nearly sparked a riot.

Besides, you didn't ask for Ethan. No one asked for Ethan. Ethan just... appeared. Like a fruit fly.

You look at him, with half a mind to say: "Did I ask for your input? No, I didn't, you prick! You sort spreadsheet columns for a living, not shipping manifests."

However, you bite your tongue while slowly minimizing your spreadsheet like you're hiding classified government intel, then reply:

"I'll keep that in mind!"

Ethan smiles like he just solved world hunger and strolls away with the smug satisfaction of a man who once read half a book on supply chain theory.

You turn back to your screen, exhale through your nose like an angry dragon, and reopen the file. You make no changes. You send the report as it is. And shockingly (*not!*)... it gets approved by leadership exactly as you had it.
You see Ethan the next day in the hallway. He gives you a thumbs-up. You smile back politely and whisper, under your breath:

"Bold choice, my ass."

What You Really Want To Say:

Get your fucking shit together

HR Approved Alternative:

Let's lean in

What You Really Want To Say:

That's the dumbest fucking idea I've ever heard

HR Approved Alternative:

I hear you. But we need to pivot.

What You Really Want To Say:

You're plain fucking wrong

HR Approved Alternative:

Devil's advocate: why wouldn't this work?

Case File

You're in a cross-departmental sync about redesigning the internal ticketing system.

The current one is so ancient, it might as well require dial-up.

Everyone agrees: it's time for an upgrade.

Then, Trevor from the purchase department speaks up.

Trevor, who rocks a Bluetooth headset like he's waiting for a call from NASA.

Trevor, whose whole aesthetic screams, "Excel, but louder."

He clears his throat and drops this gem:

"What if, instead of a digital platform, we go back to paper forms? People fill them out, drop them in a box, and then someone logs them every Friday. It's more tangible, you know?"

You blink, stare, and briefly wonder if Trevor hit his head on a supply closet shelf.

Pam from Admin chokes on her tea.

Asha from IT looks ready to file a grievance against humanity.

Internally, you're screaming: *"You're plain f*&%ing wrong, Trevor. This isn't 1993. Are we also bringing back pagers, floppy disks, and dial-up internet?!"*

But out loud, you tilt your head like you're genuinely curious and say:

"Devil's advocate: Why wouldn't this work?"

Trevor lights up.

“Well,” he begins, adjusting his Bluetooth headset like he’s about to land a plane, “Digital platforms create too much dependency on stable internet and tech literacy. Not everyone is comfortable with digital interfaces, and when things break, the entire workflow collapses. Paper is reliable. You never need to reboot paper.

He smiles like he just dropped the mic on innovation itself.

Thankfully, Asha swoops in like a hero:

“Security? Nightmare. Tracking? Impossible. Also, deforestation, anyone?”

Trevor nods thoughtfully... and never mentions paper forms again.

After the call, you sit back, gaze out the window, and whisper:

“Devil’s advocate: Why is Trevor employed?”

Holding this space to ideate synergistic blue-sky solutions for our paradigm-shifting initiatives.

What You Really Want To Say:

I'm not dealing with your BS right now

HR Approved Alternative:

Let's touch base on this

Case File

It's 9:06 a.m. on a Tuesday, and you're still mentally buffering from the weekend.

You've got *exactly* one goal today: survive until lunch without crying into your keyboard or rage-ordering stress croissants.

You're mid-email, trying to coordinate a vendor call for the eco-friendly packaging campaign launch — a months-long initiative that's been described as "the cornerstone of Q2," "a game-changer," and "the thing keeping the CMO awake at night."

Brittani from "Brand Activation," a department so mysterious you're convinced it exists solely during Q4, storms up to your desk, clutching a glittery mood board covered in magazine clippings and — wait — is that a feather?

Brittani practically vibrates with excitement. "I had this vision last night! For the launch party: an immersive jungle experience! LED parrots. Fog machines. Safari hats. And, get this — branded coconuts served with compostable straws!"

You take a minute to actually process what Brittani has just said, and you have half the mind to say:

"You know what? I'm not dealing with your BS right now. I haven't even opened Outlook yet. Also, coconuts? Really?"

But you don't. You just summon every ounce of professionalism you can muster and say, "Let's touch base after I connect with Legal."

But you know what you really mean is: *"I'm letting Legal shut this madness down so I don't have to."*

Brittani beams. "Amazing! I'll start sourcing parrots!"

She walks away humming Beyoncé, leaving you to sit there, baffled, wondering, *How does she still have a job? And where in the world did she get that feather?*

What You Really Want To Say:

Stop being a lazy fuck

HR Approved Alternative:

You're taking ownership of this

Case File

You're drowning in deadlines, eyes twitching from staring at an Excel sheet with formulas so advanced, you're half-convinced you've accidentally summoned an ancient spreadsheet deity.

Enter Darren from Finance, iced coffee in hand, strolling like he's in a rom-com montage. No urgency, and no worries.

"Hey," he says, stretching that one syllable into a full manifesto. "Quick thing—can you pull together the updated cost analysis for Q3? Shouldn't take long."

You blink. Slowly. Because you *did* pull those numbers. Last week. You color-coded the cells. You applied conditional formatting. You basically *Excel-ed* your soul into it.

But Darren didn't open the file. Darren, who's been "slammed"— aka attending MoneyFest 2025, a three-day offsite where his primary deliverable was Instagram selfies captioned "*Grind don't stop!*" and "*#FiscalAF.*"

You want to shout, "Darren, stop being a lazy f&%k and do your job. This isn't a TED Talk about coffee; it's real life."

But you've been through corporate training. You're a pro. So, instead, you take a slow, calming breath and simply say, "You're taking ownership of this."

Darren grins, completely missing the subtext. "Cool, cool. Just loop me in when it's done!"

He walks off, sipping his iced coffee like the star of a productivity parody. You, meanwhile, rename your spreadsheet *Darren's Mess (Final Final Version).xlsx*, wondering how many Darrens the workforce can sustain before total collapse.

What You Really Want To Say:

You need to fix this shit now

HR Approved Alternative:

We're on the frontline of the trenches here

10:00 a.m. All-Hands Crisis Meeting.

The client portal isn't just down — it's *error-404-your-business-is-now-doomed* down.

Clients are spiraling. Emails are flooding in. The team is panicking.

And Dylan from IT?

Nowhere to be found.

After a frantic hunt, you find him in the breakroom, casually munching on a burrito the size of a small child — because, of course, Dylan operates on burrito time, not crisis time.

You — with a tight jaw — "Dylan. The portal. It's been down for an hour. Clients are losing their minds."

Dylan responds — mouth full, zero urgency — "Eh, yeah. Probably just a server hiccup. I'll get to it after this burrito. Gotta carb up for peak performance, you know?"

You, of course, want to scream, "DYLAN, YOU NEED TO FIX THIS SH*T NOW OR I'M REPLACING YOU WITH A CHATBOT THAT RESPECTS DEADLINES."

But instead, channeling the calm fury of a seasoned office warrior, you say: "Dylan, we're in the trenches here. Clients are actively losing it. Can we microwave the burrito later?"

Dylan sighs dramatically, as though he's the one suffering.

"Fine, fine. But after this, I'm definitely clocking out for lunch."

You nod, already mentally drafting a job posting titled:

IT Specialist Wanted – Must Prioritize Servers Over Snacks.

What You Really Want To Say:

You think any of us are happy being here on a Friday night?

HR Approved Alternative:

We're a family

Case File

It's a Friday night, and you're at the office.

Somewhere in the world, people are clinking glasses, eating tacos, and not wearing lanyards.

But not you. Not your team.

Nope.

You're crammed in Conference Room B —a room that smells permanently of burnt coffee and regret — huddled around a flickering monitor.

The client presentation is due Monday morning, and Natalie from Events just dropped the bomb: her entire pitch deck is in Papyrus.

Natalie, in a panicked voice, begins, "I don't understand. It looked fine on my laptop!"

You're feeling dead inside as you reply, "You've had this since Tuesday."

Natalie, teary-eyed, clutching an oat milk latte like it's an emotional support beverage, says, "Yeah, but Tuesday was, like, really hard for me."

You survey the room: Tom's on his fifth Red Bull, visibly vibrating; Asha hasn't blinked in hours, and Jared from Legal? Fully asleep. Mouth open. Snoring.

Then Natalie drops the kicker: "I just don't think it's fair that I have to stay late to fix this."

Oh no. Ohhh no no no.

You want to shout:

Fair? Natalie, you think any of us are happy being here on a Friday night? None of us wants to be here. It's Friday, for Pete's sake! My tacos are gone. My soul is gone. We all died at 6 PM.

But that's not what you scream. Nah.

What you actually say (with the calm fury of a motivational speaker on their last nerve) is:

"Look, Natalie... we're a family. And families support each other, through it all, right?"

Natalie nods, finally switching to the acceptable font.

Tom cheers, Asha blinks, and Jared stirs from his nap.

This page is disrupting the traditional content paradigm through strategic absence.

What You Really Want To Say:

This report is completely useless

HR Approved Alternative:

Can you take a second look at this? Also if you can drill it down, that'd be great

Case File

It's the weekly sales review, and Brad hands you his "comprehensive" Q2 sales report. It's 47 pages long, which feels promising—until you open it.

The intro? Three pages of corporate fluff. There are 12 unlabeled charts that seem like they're based on guesswork rather than data. And Slide 26? A blurry screenshot of... something. Excel? A haunted house? You're not sure.

The final takeaway? "Sales are... happening."

Meanwhile, Brad's sitting back in his chair, proud, like he's just solved world peace. You stare at him and are tempted to ask:

"Brad, did your cat walk across the keyboard? Did you bribe a raccoon to build these slides? Because this report is useless! Believe me, I've seen more insight on a Snapple cap!"

But you're a professional. And we don't do that here. So, you clutch your reusable cup like it's a life raft, and in a calm voice, you say:

"Brad, thanks for putting this together! Can you take another look at it, though? Also, if you can drill it down, that'd be great. Just... distill the key points. And maybe try to use some actual words instead of abstract concepts, if you could."

Brad nods seriously, as if you've spoken in code, and obliviously fires up PowerPoint again.

"Totally! I'll add more... data stuff."

You smile and nod while dying a little inside.

What You Really Want To Say:

You're in a world of trouble now

HR Approved Alternative:

Have you got a minute for a quick chat?

What You Really Want To Say:

WTF are you talking about?

HR Approved Alternative:

A lot to unpack here

What You Really Want To Say:

You've fucked this up... again?

HR Approved Alternative:

Let's establish a process

It's Thursday, 3:22 p.m., and the client pitch is in an hour.

It's the final deadline—well, the third final deadline because someone keeps "just making a few tweaks." You haven't slept properly in days. You're 70% caffeine, 30% simmering rage. And this slide deck? It's been through 12 versions. *Twelve*. At this point, it probably qualifies for a pension.

You open the file that Eric from Marketing swore—keyword being swore—was polished, proofed, and ready to dazzle.

You click on Slide 1, but it's the wrong client's name. Slide 2? Their competitor's logo. Slide 3? A dolphin. Not a clever metaphor. Not a client mascot. Just a full-screen photo of a dolphin smiling like it knows something you don't.

You blink and rub your eyes. Then, you click on the third slide again.

Yep! Still there. Still very aquatic.

Slowly, you swivel in your chair and turn to Eric, who is casually munching pretzels like he didn't just upload a PowerPoint straight out of a fever dream. You desperately want to say:

"Eric. You've f*&ked this up... again? Are you running a side hustle in sabotage?"

But you don't. Because Eric would report you for being "aggressive" at work. Therefore, you calmly say:

"Okay... let's establish a process moving forward—something simple, like... making sure the deck doesn't include marine life or logos that could tank the account."

Eric looks up mid-crunch and laughs.
"Oh weird! Maybe I uploaded the wrong version. I had, like, four open. Haha."

You do not echo that "haha." Instead, you open your backup file (*Final_Final_ActualFinal_THISONEv2.pptx*) and start fixing every slide. Again. Dolphin? Deleted. Company reputation? Saved.

Eric, still blissfully employed, wanders off, pretzels in hand.

What You Really Want To Say:

I've got enough shit to deal with

HR Approved Alternative:

I don't have the bandwidth right now

What You Really Want To Say:

That was one very stupid suggestion

HR Approved Alternative:

I'm looking for more of a paradigm shift

What You Really Want To Say:

Stop fucking doodling

HR Approved Alternative:

Would you like to chime in?

Case File

It's another team brainstorming session.

The goal? A productive meeting about the upcoming product launch.

The reality? It's shaping up to be either a disaster or your villain origin story.

You scan the room. Metrics and market strategies are being debated—but not by Anna from Finance. You know she's usually sharp, but right now, she's staring blankly at the projector screen.

In fact, she's not even pretending to pay attention to the discussion. No, Anna is deep in what can only be described as a doodle trance.

Her pen swirls across her notepad with an intensity that suggests she's sketching the meaning of life itself. Is it a flower? A cat? An abstract cry for help?

Whatever it is, it's getting alarmingly detailed while the rest of the team struggles through sales projections.

You've had enough. Anna's Picasso moment feels like a subtle protest—or a sign she's seconds away from losing it in this corporate circus.

You briefly consider saying:

Anna, stop f%king doodling and focus! You're not prepping for an art exhibit, and the only thing you're drawing is your career exit strategy.*

But you don't want to be rude, so you simply opt to say:

"Anna, would you like to chime in? You've been very... inspired over there."

You're hoping she'll get that you mean:

Okay, Anna. Put the pen down before I lose what's left of my sanity. Maybe contribute instead of designing the next frustrated employee art trend.

Anna looks up, blinking like she just realized other humans exist.

Her face lights up as though she's about to deliver a life-altering insight.

Instead, she says:

Oh! Sorry, I was just—uh, well, I think I can explain this later. But this could totally be the next corporate logo. Like... funkier, you know?

You take a long, deep breath, suppressing the urge to launch the projector remote into orbit. "I'll keep that in mind, Anna. Maybe we'll discuss it... during the next finance meeting."

She nods, entirely unbothered, and goes back to doodling.

As the meeting limps along, you glance at Anna's growing masterpiece and wonder if it's a metaphor for your life: surrounded by chaos, barely holding it together, while someone else turns their notepad into a stress-induced art gallery.

HR has deleted this page for being too offensive.

It was really, really good.

What You Really Want To Say:

I'm not in the mood for this crap

HR Approved Alternative:

Let's put a pin on that one

Case File

You're in the home stretch. The weekend is so close you can practically taste the Pinot Grigio waiting in your fridge. Just five more minutes of this meeting, which stands between you and sweet freedom. That's when IT's resident tech shaman, Steve, clears his throat with the gravitas of someone about to reveal the meaning of life.

"I've been running diagnostics on our bandwidth pain points," he begins, his eyes gleaming. "What if we... migrate to a mesh network topology?"

You know this song:

- **Verse 1:** Steve's "revolutionary idea" (aka, the same pitch as last month).
- **Chorus:** Vague promises of "seamless connectivity."
- **Bridge:** Everyone pretends to care.
- **Outro:** Nothing actually changes.

You're standing there, nodding politely, trying your hardest not to let your eyes glaze over because there's no part of you that's even remotely interested in what he's saying. You don't care. You've been dealing with Steve's endless technical tangents for months, and you just can't take it anymore.

You're a moment away from saying:
"Steve, I'm not in the mood for this crap. Your last "foolproof solution" made the printer scream like a banshee every time someone sent a PDF.

But what you actually say, forcing all emotion out of your voice, is: "Fascinating! Let's put a pin in that one and revisit when we're all... *fresher*."

You're hoping he'll catch onto the sarcasm. However, he doesn't notice your internal struggle. In fact, he's already scribbling more notes, preparing to email everyone about the details of his "incredible idea" after this meeting.

As the meeting finally ends, you make record time sprinting to the elevator, only to hear Steve call after you:

"Wait! Did I mention the blockchain integration possibility?!"
You jab the "close door" button with religious fervor.

Somewhere, a wine bottle pops its cork in solidarity.

What You Really Want To Say:

Just fucking figure it out

HR Approved Alternative:

Please champion this project

Case File

It's Thursday afternoon, and the office is buzzing as everyone scrambles to wrap up projects before the weekend. You're on the phone with Tom, a junior team member who just doesn't get it. Tom loves the sound of his own voice—and apparently hates Google, because every question he asks could be solved in 0.3 seconds with a search bar.

Today's crisis? Step four of a task you've walked him through three times. You sent him step-by-step instructions. You even made him a guide worthy of a museum display. And now, 30 minutes into the call, Tom is still confused.

You're low on patience. Lower on caffeine. And Tom's endless confusion is the cherry on top of an already frustrating day. You want to verbally lash out and say:

"Tom, just f%*king figure it out. I've explained this 50 times. Use your brain, stop calling me, and handle it—it's not rocket science!"

But you remember he's still a junior, so instead, you manage to keep your tone even and say:

"Tom, I need you to champion this project. I'm confident you can take the reins and drive it home."

Hopefully, he'll get that you mean: *Tom, please, for the love of all that is holy, take responsibility. I'm not your babysitter. I'm two seconds away from assigning you to organize paper clips full-time.*

As you get back to work, you wonder how long it'll be before Tom accidentally emails the entire company asking how to attach a file again.

What You Really Want To Say:

Yeah I'm not reading all of that

HR Approved Alternative:

Let's take a high level look at the documents

What You Really Want To Say:

Stop pretending to work and actually do something

HR Approved Alternative:

We all need to have some skin in the game

What You Really Want To Say:

That was quite the fuck up. You're going to need to plead for mercy.

HR Approved Alternative:

You should reach out to John

Case File

You walk into what can only be described as a corporate disaster zone. Raul from Sales is frozen in front of the projector, his PowerPoint presentation still beaming proudly on the screen:

Corporate Sales Strategy (Followed immediately by an accidental screenshot of his Tinder messages)

The client — a major account responsible for 45% of revenue — is sitting there, eyes wide, with the expression of someone who just witnessed a car crash in slow motion. The last visible message on the screen reads: "You up? (with a peach and water-splash emoji)."

What you know is that:

- Raul was "just quickly checking his phone" before the meeting.
- He somehow managed to share his entire screen instead of his carefully prepared presentation.

The client's VP of Finance is quietly massaging his temples like he's trying to erase the last few minutes from his memory.

You want to shake your head and say:

"Raul, that was quite the f*&k up. You're going to need to plead for mercy. Start writing your will. I hear HR is looking for volunteers for the next Mars mission — maybe you can hitch a ride."

But you can't say that. So, you close the laptop and say:

"Raul, you should reach out to John. Right now."

You're hoping that your tone and eyes will convey that: *John in Legal is the only one who can possibly clean up this mess. Even then, it's a Hail Mary. Time to start praying, buddy.*

Raul, looking like he's seen a ghost, mutters:

"John... in Legal?"

You nod, your face dead serious, as if you're giving him the last piece of advice he'll ever need.

The client's VP of Finance stands up, stares at the screen one last time, and delivers the five most soul-crushing words in corporate history:

"We'll be in touch. Maybe."

As the door shuts behind them, Raul finally unfreezes, his face pale and trembling.

"So... bad?"

You hand him John's business card without a word, like it's his last hope.

"Tell him you're willing to relocate. Anywhere. Preferably off-planet."

This page is awaiting approval from HR.

Estimated Wait Time: Forever.

What You Really Want To Say:

Why am I even in this meeting?

HR Approved Alternative:

I'd just like to piggyback off what you said

What You Really Want To Say:

Get the fuck out of here

HR Approved Alternative:

Let's table this for now and circle back to it later

What You Really Want To Say:

Stop fucking around

HR Approved Alternative:

It's time to hit the ground running

Case File

It's Monday morning. You've just returned from a long weekend — three glorious days away from your inbox, Slack notifications, and the soul-sapping sound of your coworker's Bluetooth headset beeping every time she unmutes.

You're still mildly sunburnt, emotionally attached to your out-of-office reply, and spiritually unprepared for what lies ahead.

But reality hits hard. Your calendar? Triple-booked. Your to-do list? A novella. And your team? Standing around like NPCs waiting for a quest.

Enter Cody, the human embodiment of "delay."

Cody is supposed to be leading the new product launch this week — you know, the one that's already been postponed twice because someone "accidentally deleted the asset folder" (spoiler alert: it was Cody).

He strolls in 20 minutes late, iced mocha in one hand and what appears to be a half-eaten croissant in the other. He's wearing sunglasses indoors because, apparently, Cody's fresh from headlining Coachella.

You attempt professionalism: "Morning, everyone. We've got a lot to get through today—"

Cody interrupts you like it's his show. "Yeah, yeah, but first — what if we kicked this off with a little game? Something light. I saw this TikTok where teams draw their aura using crayons!"

You blink. Slowly. Twice. Because surely this is a joke. *Crayons? Auras? On launch week?*

The rest of the team chuckles nervously, like they're unsure whether to laugh or cry. You? You're gripping your reusable coffee cup like it's a stress ball.

One glance at the overflowing task list, the looming deadline, and the document titled:

URGENT_FINAL_FINAL_LAUNCH_NOW_REALLYTHISONE

... and it's safe to say you're at your limit.

You're five seconds from shouting:

"Cody, stop f*%king around! This isn't art class. There is no aura. There are only deliverables. Focus before I revoke your coffee privileges."

But at the last second, you remember the HR policy against profanity in the workplace, so you clear your throat and say:

"Alright, team, it's time to hit the ground running. First things first..."

You say this with a smile, but your eyes are doing most of the heavy lifting.

Cody shrugs, clearly not reading the room, and says, "Totally. Let's run fast and draw our energy colors later, yeah?"

You don't respond. You just pull up the project board, drag the deadline forward by two days, and silently pray to the gods of productivity to intervene.

As the meeting begins and Cody finally opens his laptop — probably to watch more TikToks — you lean back in your chair and think:

I should've extended my leave. Permanently.

Blank due to unforeseen budget cuts.

Feel free to thank management.

What You Really Want To Say:

I'm sick of doing unpaid overtime

HR Approved Alternative:

I'd like to touch base on establishing some work-life balance

Case File

It's 6:45 a.m. on a Saturday.

You're in the middle of nowhere, sitting in a rundown hotel room with peeling wallpaper and fluorescent lights that hum like they're actively trying to destroy your soul.

The AC in the room broke three hours ago, and you're now covered in sweat that's not only from the heat but from the crushing realization that you're here for "Camp Synergy" — the company's retreat.

More accurately, you're here because skipping the retreat wasn't really an option. Attendance was "strongly encouraged," which everyone knows is code for mandatory, because heaven forbid you prioritize rest over "team synergy."

Opting out would've been quietly noted (read: career-limiting move), so now you're donating your weekend to unpaid corporate bonding disguised as professional development.

Your only companions are a flimsy company-branded T-shirt and Brenda from HR, who's already done five sun salutations in the hallway and is now sipping from a "Rise and Grind" Yeti tumbler.

You were hoping to have a weekend where you could, you know, sleep in.

Maybe check your email on "silent mode" so your boss wouldn't be able to ping you about that deadline that's "super urgent," even though it's been on your calendar for two weeks.

But instead, you're trapped here for "Team Building" activities that make you want to fake an injury just to escape.

Brenda claps loudly to get everyone's attention. "Okay, team! Before our morning gratitude hike, we're doing a silent journal exercise about 'what work means to our souls!'"

You glance at the sticky notes in front of you. The words blur together as the heat in the room rises.

Your soul? It's somewhere between the sticky floor and the smell of microwaved breakfast sandwiches.

Behind you, Karen from Sales is arguing with the hotel staff about the coffee machine that "isn't working properly," despite the fact that it's not even 7:00 a.m. and you can already hear the faint sound of a "team-building" icebreaker happening in the parking lot.

You know that you only have two choices:

- Scream into the woods like a corporate banshee and risk being written up for "excessive emotional expression," or
- Swallow your rage and try to say something appropriately professional.

You can already envision how the first choice will go, and it will involve you screaming something like:

Brenda, I'm sick of doing unpaid overtime. I spent nine hours last night fixing Don's spreadsheet while you were all bonding over wine and trust falls! Now it's barely morning, and you have me stuck in a damp, poorly-ventilated hotel conference room, reflecting on my soul?! My soul is tired. *My soul wants to be left alone, not scribbling in a journal like I'm an unpaid intern!*

But, instead of raising your voice in front of the entire team (and making it awkward for everyone), you take a deep breath and say:

"You know, Brenda, I'd really love to touch base about establishing some work-life balance. I think it'd really help us show up more energized and productive."

It seems like the message flies right above her head, though, because in the next instant, she says: "Exactly! That's why we're doing gratitude yoga at lunch! Nothing says work-life balance like downward dog in 90-degree heat while wearing company swag!"

You nod slowly, making a mental note to expense this entire trip under "emotional hazard pay" — and to finally update your resume.

This page has been deleted by legal.

We just wrote what everyone was already thinking.

What You Really Want To Say:

Get off your lazy butt

HR Approved Alternative:

We need to show a sense of urgency in our work

You're deep in the trenches of a team deadline that's been creeping toward you like a slow-motion train wreck.

The group chat has been popping off all day — slides being finalized, data being double-checked, everyone triple-guessing their Excel formulas because last quarter's disaster is still a fresh wound.

Everyone's stressed. Everyone's focused.

Everyone, that is, except Craig.

Craig — mid-40s, owns a small assortment of fleece vests, and has somehow built a reputation for "thinking big" while doing absolutely nothing.

He's been sitting in the corner of the open-plan office for the last three hours, casually watching LinkedIn tutorials at full volume and giving unsolicited tips like:

Maybe we should start the deck with a quote about leadership? (No one asked, Craig.)

You've now written 90% of the presentation, coordinated input from the data team, edited everyone's slides, and manually resized three logos because Craig couldn't figure out how to stop stretching them into oblivion.

And what's Craig doing now?

Eating a cup of yogurt. Loudly. With his AirPods in while watching a TED Talk about "productivity."

You just want to storm over to him, pull out his AirPods, and say:

Craig. Get off your lazy butt. If I have to carry this team one more time, I'm gonna have them put my name on the company building.

But you don't.

You spin around in your chair, crack your knuckles, and channel your inner middle manager, then say:

“Hey Craig, we really need to show a sense of urgency in our work right now — could you please take the lead on compiling the final summary slides?”

Craig blinks. Slowly.

Then nods like you just handed him the Olympic torch.

“Yeah, yeah. I can take that on. Just give me a few to, uh... circle back.”

He opens PowerPoint. Stares at it like he’s never seen a slide before.

Then — naturally — asks, “So... like, what's the final content we're including?”

You stare at him, dead inside.

“The same content that’s been in the deck for the last hour, Craig.”

The intern in the corner quietly messages you:

"If he asks about content again, I’m going to flip a whiteboard."

This page has pivoted to a whitespace-first approach to robustly engage core stakeholders and unlock agile, solution-oriented ecosystems.

What You Really Want To Say:

It's almost the weekend. Time to coast along.

HR Approved Alternative:

Let's prioritize the low-hanging fruit

The clock ticks dangerously close to 4:00 p.m. on a Friday, and the weekend is beckoning you over. Across the room, Maya from Project Management is doing that thing where she stands up suddenly like she's about to announce the cure for cancer, but it's always just another "quick sync." This time, she's waving a whiteboard marker like a conductor's baton.

"Team!" she begins. "We need to sprint through these last action items before EOD!"

You glance at your to-do list, which currently reads:

- Pretend to update the CRM.
- Delete old emails (self-preservation).
- Practice your "I'm definitely working" face for when the boss walks by.

You feel like saying:
"Maya, it's almost the weekend. Time to coast along like a grocery cart with a wobbly wheel. Nobody's sprinting anywhere except to the bar."
But because corporate life has trained you better than to speak your mind too openly, you instead nod thoughtfully and say:
"You're so right, Maya. Let's prioritize the low-hanging fruit first."

The underlying meaning? *I will be "researching industry benchmarks" (watching cat videos) until 4:30 p.m., at which point I will become one with the exit door.*

Maya, ever the optimist, claps her hands.

"Great point! Let's tackle the easy wins!"

She gestures to the whiteboard, where she's written "*OUR PENETRATION STRATEGY*" in all caps, followed by three bullet points that all say "*SYNERGY*" in slightly different colors. You smile, open a spreadsheet titled "*URGENT METRICS*," and immediately minimize it to check the clock again. Three minutes closer to freedom.

Maya, oblivious, is now diagramming something with far too many arrows. You nod along, mentally calculating how many snacks you can fit in your bag for the escape. The weekend is so close you can taste it—and unlike Maya's "action items," it's going to be delicious.

What You Really Want To Say:

Stop dumping shit on me at the last minute

HR Approved Alternative:

I’d really appreciate it if you gave me a bit more notice for tasks like so I can focus on delivering quality work

Case File

You're in the middle of your daily "pretending to look busy while actually planning dinner" ritual when Tiffany from Client Relations materializes at your desk with that particular brand of manic cheer that always precedes disaster. Her smile is wide, her energy drink is half-empty, and her tote bag says "I'm Not Bossy, I Just Have Better Ideas" in an aggressively curly font.

"Hey, superstar!" she chirps, dropping a 47-page document on your keyboard. "The Anderson account needs a tiny refresh before their 3:30 p.m. call today. Just some light proofing, a few formatting tweaks, and maybe a complete overhaul of the financial projections? You're the best!"

You stare at the document. The "tiny refresh" includes:

- rewriting six months of client notes that Tiffany apparently took in hieroglyphics.
- rebuilding an entire pricing model because someone (Tiffany) used the "buy one, get one free" formula from her weekend couponing.
- a sticky note that says "Make it pop!" with no further instructions.

You consider saying:

"Tiffany, stop dumping sh*t on me at the last minute. This isn't a 'quick favor,' this is a hostage situation. The only thing that's going to 'pop' is my sanity."

But you don't. Instead, with the tranquility of a yoga instructor on Xanax, you say:

"Tiffany, I'd really appreciate it if you gave me a bit more notice for tasks like this so I can focus on delivering quality work. Instead of... whatever this is."

Tiffany blinks like you've just insulted her.

"But it's just polishing! Like, 20 minutes max!" She says this with the confidence of someone who has never actually opened a spreadsheet.

What You Really Want To Say:

You are the fucking problem

HR Approved Alternative:

There seems to be an issue with the current approach

It's Tuesday morning. You're on your fourth Zoom call of the day, and it's not even 11 a.m.

Yet somehow, your blood pressure has reached the same level it does when your mom says, "I saw something on Facebook..."

At the center of the chaos? Vanessa from Ops.

Vanessa, who speaks exclusively in vague buzzwords like "streamline," "value-add," and "synergistic efficiency," while saying nothing of actual substance.

Vanessa, who once "accidentally" deleted the team's shared drive, then followed up with a GIF of a puppy in sunglasses captioned "Stay PAWsome!"

Vanessa, who insists she's a "big picture thinker," which really means she avoids actual work by turning it into abstract poetry.

Today's meeting? A post-mortem on a client pitch that nosedived so hard it left a crater in the company's reputation.

Everyone knows why it failed: Vanessa.

She hijacked the deck with her "visionary pivot," didn't send the final slides until four minutes before the meeting – literally as people were clicking "Join" and then proceeded to talk over the client's CFO like she was giving a speech no one asked for.

And now? Vanessa – completely straight-faced – chimes in:

"I think we need to reassess the team's commitment to the strategy. The execution didn't reflect our core objectives."

You stare at your screen in disbelief, wondering if this is what it feels like to astral project out of your body or if you're just hallucinating. Vanessa is calmly shifting the blame onto literally everyone else, including the intern, who wasn't even on the project.

You really want to unmute your mic and give her a piece of your mind with a few words:

"Vanessa. Hold up! *You* are the f*%king problem. This project didn't fail because of 'execution' — it failed because your 'strategy' was built entirely out of LinkedIn jargon and unchecked delusion."

But then you can't say that, can you? You'd get fired before you even had a chance to get your daughter that stuffed puppy she's been looking forward to all month. So, you simply unmute your mic and say:

"Vanessa, there seems to be an issue with the current approach. Maybe we can revisit some of the assumptions we made going in?"

Vanessa nods thoughtfully and says, "Exactly! I felt like I was the only one aligned with the vision."

You mute yourself to hold off from saying anything further. Maybe you even turn off your camera for a few seconds so you can nonchalantly scream quietly into a pillow.

The meeting finally ends, and you immediately send a private message to your coworker slash drinking buddy, James in Marketing:

"New drinking game: Take a shot every time Vanessa uses 'alignment' to dodge accountability."

He replies with just one word:

"Hospital."

This page is leveraging whitespace to enhance cross-functional visibility.

What You Really Want To Say:

I know how to do my fucking job

HR Approved Alternative:

I like things done in a particular way

Case File

You’ve just wrapped up an intense, hour-long team call about yet another "urgent" client request.

You’re tired, but for the first time all day, things feel under control. Tasks? Delegated. Team? Aligned. Inbox? Blessedly calm.

And then Gary from Finance strides in.

Gary, the unofficial president of “Unsolicited Opinions, Inc.”

He’s the type who’d RSVP to a potluck, show up with a single bag of chips, and still lecture everyone on how to plate their casseroles.

Somehow, Gary’s managed to gather just enough knowledge about your job to be both dangerous and infuriating.

Today’s masterpiece?

He stands, hands on hips, with the smug confidence of someone who’s never managed a deadline in their life.

"Hey, I was thinking about the budget for the new campaign. Have you considered reworking the timeline to avoid the end-of-month crunch? Just wondering if you've thought about it from a financial perspective.”

You can feel your blood pressure spike.

Gary, of course, thinks a “suggestion” is actually a 12-step mandate that involves spreadsheets, pivot tables, and possibly an interpretive dance of inefficiency.

You're tempted to snap:

“Gary. I know how to do my f*%king job. You don’t need to ‘advise’ me on my role. You’re not the one balancing deadlines and budgets; I am. You keep handling the spreadsheets; I’ve got this.”

Because, honestly, you do.

You've done this a thousand times, and if you had a dime for every time Gary thought he could "improve" something, you'd be living in a beach house by now.

But you don't snap. No. You take a deep breath, and say:

"Gary, I appreciate the input. However, I like things done in a particular way, and we've already set a plan in motion. I'm confident the timeline will work as is."

Gary, clearly not hearing the subtle hint, gives you a look that screams, "I'm smarter than you."

He scribbles something down in his notebook and says, "Okay, just checking! I'll keep an eye on the numbers, just in case you need some backup."

Backup? From Gary? Sure.

You nod politely, keeping the smile on your face while your soul screams internally.

As Gary walks away, you try to hold back the urge to send him an email titled: *Re: Stop Micromanaging My Department.*

You immediately open your calendar and schedule a "catch-up" with your boss. The meeting title? *How to survive Gary's Process Improvements Without Moving to a New Career (or Universe).*

Because if Gary's going to keep "improving" processes, you're going to need either a therapist or a spreadsheet exorcist.

Reserved for synergizing key learnings and actionable insights at scale.

What You Really Want To Say:

I really don't care

HR Approved Alternative:

Let's take this offline

Case File

It's mid-afternoon on a Wednesday. Productivity? Nonexistent. Your phone is buzzing with calendar reminders for meetings you don't remember scheduling. Your inbox? Pinging so relentlessly, it's like a mini alarm clock reminding you that your sanity is slipping away, one "Quick Question" email at a time.

You open the latest offender, subject line: *Quick Question About the TPS Reports*.

It's from Mike in Marketing. Mike, who has somehow mastered the art of "checking in" about things that don't actually need checking in. Mike, whose unofficial job title might as well be "Inbox Stuffing Specialist."

You click the email. It's a one-liner that, under normal circumstances, would've been a 30-second conversation. Instead, Mike's gone ahead and looped in the entire team:

"Hey, just wanted to confirm, the font for the TPS reports is Calibri, right? Also, should we include the quarterly performance summary in section 3 or 4?"

You stare at the screen, unblinking, as your last shred of patience packs its bags and books a one-way ticket far away. The sheer magnitude of this question is overwhelming in its lack of significance. Mike's question could be answered by simply looking at the document. Yet here he is, bringing the whole team into a trivial debate that doesn't need a second thought.

Your first thought? To type back:

"Mike, I truly do not care about this font debate. Pick one, flip a coin, let your cat decide—I really don't care. Just stop wasting everyone's time. Also, please unclog my inbox before I start replying to your emails with memes."

But saying that would surely open the floodgates for more unnecessary emails from Mike. So, you settle for the professional response:

"Hey Mike, let's take this offline. Let me know if you need any help finalizing it."

You hit "Send" and immediately resume real work.

The worst part? You know this isn't the last time you'll hear from Mike today. He's probably already drafting an email about "synergy" that'll hit your inbox five minutes after this one.

What You Really Want To Say:

I hate you

HR Approved Alternative:

I'm not seeing a good fit here

What You Really Want To Say:

Get lost. I'm having a moment here.

HR Approved Alternative:

I'll ping you the details later

What You Really Want To Say:

Another harebrained idea from Einstein here

HR Approved Alternative:

Let's focus on real-world solutions here

It's 10:04 a.m., and you're four minutes into what was supposed to be a quick 15-minute stand-up. You're already regretting not pretending to have a dentist appointment.

In strolls Blake from Product Development. Blake, who once tried to "gamify" the paid time off request system by turning it into a leaderboard. Today, he's back with a new "brilliant" idea: a new company initiative where clients "earn discounts" by completing daily riddles.

Blake, eyes wide with excitement and holding a half-drunk protein shake, goes, "What if we made all our onboarding emails rhyme? Like, turn them into a treasure hunt! People love puzzles."

You hear someone gasp. It's Marcus, the intern. Probably just realizing Blake is, in fact, not joking.

Then, Blake turns to the whiteboard. In a rush of untamed energy, he starts sketching out a flowchart that looks suspiciously like a pirate map. It has dotted lines, looping paths, and an oversized "X" labeled "Client Loyalty." He explains that each riddle solved would bring clients one step closer to exclusive discounts—"like a digital treasure hunt for engagement." You suddenly realize this isn't just a pitch—it's the next installment in his quest to gamify the entire company experience.

You're thinking (probably even saying it internally): *Oh, dear. Another harebrained idea from Einstein here. What's next, onboarding by smoke signal?*

But out loud? You shake your head a little and say:

"Let's focus on real-world solutions here."

Blake nods slowly, then adds, "Okay, but what if we compromise with a limerick series?"

You sip from your water bottle so aggressively that it should count as a complaint.

What You Really Want To Say:

No one really cares about this project but I'm going to pretend to do something

HR Approved Alternative:

I'll run it up the flagpole

You're halfway through Wednesday. You're at your desk, staring blankly at your screen, trying to summon the will to pretend to be busy.

That's when Samantha, the self-proclaimed "Innovation Shaman," materializes in a cloud of essential oils and misplaced enthusiasm.

She's clutching a three-ring binder labeled "Disruptive File Taxonomy" like it's the goddamn Rosetta Stone, and her eyes have that particular manic gleam of someone who's just discovered the power of sticky notes.

"Okay, hear me out," she says, slapping down a laminated color wheel titled: *File Naming Feng Shui.* "What if we rebrand all our shared folders to spark joy? Instead of the 'Annual Budget,' we could have... 'Coin Carnival'! And 'Client Contracts' becomes 'The Deal Den!'" She pauses, waiting for your mind to be blown.

You're bored out of your mind and thinking, *Samantha, no one cares about this project. Not the interns, not the janitors, and not even the office spider that lives behind the ficus by the reception area. I would rather lick a printer cartridge than spend one second "gamifying" file paths. But I'm going to pretend to do something so I can get back to doom-scrolling in peace.*

However, you don't share your thoughts. Nope. Instead, you nod like you completely understand, even though your brain just walked out the door, and say:

"Wow, Samantha! This is... bold. I'll run it up the flagpole and see what leadership thinks!"

Samantha claps her hands and leaves happily. You wait until she's out of sight, then immediately hit up IT on Slack:

"Can you disable my access to shared drives? For... security reasons."

What You Really Want To Say:

Are we even speaking the same fucking language?

HR Approved Alternative:

Let's try to get on the same page

Case File

You're trapped in a Zoom call that somehow combines the excitement of watching paint dry with the intellectual stimulation of reading a microwave manual.

On screen, Pete from "Strategic Synergy Enablement" (a department that definitely doesn't need to exist) is mid-flowchart, using words that sound impressive but mean absolutely nothing.

"If we can leverage the synergies of our ideation ecosystem to fast-track deliverables, we'll be able to loop in vertical stakeholders and really drive some blue-sky outcomes."

You've been nodding so long that your neck has officially given up. Your camera is off, your mic is muted, and you're currently researching "how to fake a Wi-Fi outage without getting caught."

Pete pauses for dramatic effect. "So, if you could just pivot the actionables into a proactive vision deck using agile mindfulness principles, that'd be great... sound good?"

You stare blankly. *Is this English? Is anyone taking notes? Is this a prank?*

You're highly tempted to say: *Pete, are we even speaking the same f*%king language? I've heard of fortune cookies with more substance than this meeting.*

But what you actually say, with the enthusiasm of a hostage reading a ransom note, is: "Hold on, Pete. Let's try to get on the same page. Maybe we can simplify the approach?"

Pete nods and says: "Perfect! I'll socialize a beta pilot road map and circle back with a disruptive thought leadership framework!"

As the meeting ends, you're left thinking: *Is "thought leadership framework" just code for "I made this up in the shower"?*

What You Really Want To Say:

Stop changing your bloody mind every minute

HR Approved Alternative:

Can I get some clarification on the scope if we're going to be making some adjustments?

Case File

It's Monday morning, and you've already updated the client deck three times before your laptop even finished syncing. Sitting across from you in the conference room is Eliza, the VP of "Creative Alignment," who has changed the direction of this project so many times that it now qualifies as a weather pattern.

On Friday, she wanted it bold and punchy. By Sunday (yes, she emailed you on a Sunday), it was all about "minimalism and quiet luxury." Now, in this 9 a.m. meeting, she's holding up a mood board filled with pictures of clouds and whispering, "I'm feeling something more... *elemental.* Like, less structure, more sensation."

You've redone this presentation so many times that you're starting to forget what it was supposed to be about in the first place. And yet Eliza, with a smoothie in one hand and boundless creative energy in the other, continues:

"Actually, let's go back to the first version... but merge in pieces of the third... and maybe make the whole thing vertical? And let's shift the palette to 'gentle dusk'—you know, that feeling between a soft sigh and the moment before a thought forms?"

You have an urge to headbutt the whiteboard and say:

"Stop changing your goddamn mind every minute. My Google Slides history is starting to look like a crime scene!"

But instead, you inhale and let out the deepest sigh you've ever sighed, and respond:

"Can I get some clarification on the scope if we're going to be making some adjustments?"

Eliza nods enthusiastically, completely unaware that your polite phrasing is really just the grown-up version of screaming into a pillow.

What You Really Want To Say:

What in the actual fuck is this horseshit?

HR Approved Alternative:

This is not a bad start, but I think it could use some fine-tuning. Let's go over it together.

Case File

It's 4:57 p.m. on a Thursday, and you are three minutes away from a guilt-free scroll through holiday rentals.

However, you get a Slack ping from Callum, the junior analyst who once proudly said Excel was "kinda like Canva, right?"

Against your better judgment, you open the file he's sent — a report that looks less like a quarterly performance summary and more like a high school group project cobbled together the night before it was due.

The bar charts are missing labels. The pie chart somehow has eight slices for four categories.

And instead of proper figures, he's written "a lot" next to revenue and "not great" under expenses. There's even an emoji of a rocket ship next to the Q3 projections.

You rub your temples, rereading the slide titled *Quarterly Wins*. There are no wins. The document is such a disaster that it should come with a bright yellow warning triangle and a siren sound effect.

You're frozen — and not in awe. Your first instinct is to say:

"What in the actual f*%k is this horseshit?"

But you remember you're a professional, so you channel every drop of professional patience into your soul and comment:

"This is not a bad start, but I think it could use some fine-tuning. Let's go over it together."

Callum, clearly proud of his visual masterpiece, replies:

"Oh great! I wasn't sure if the rocket was too much."

You smile through gritted teeth and mutter, "Oh no, Callum. The rocket's perfect. Let's launch... right into the editing."

What You Really Want To Say:

Have you lost your mind? This is mental.

HR Approved Alternative:

I'm having a hard time understanding your logic. Can you explain the thought process behind this?

It's Monday morning, and you're still shaking off the fog of the weekend, when Liam from marketing barrels into the team meeting with the kind of energy only someone who micro-doses chaos can bring.

With a grin on his face, he slaps a laminated mood board onto the table like he just invented sliced bread.

"New campaign idea," he announces proudly. "We rebrand our financial planning app... as a lifestyle guru. Like, emotionally intelligent budgeting. We give the app a name — like Tom. Tom helps you feel your finances."

You blink. Hard. You're not sure what's worse — the idea itself or the fact that the title slide has a cartoon character in a tiny blazer giving a thumbs up.

The tagline? Tom (the app, mind you) says, "Don't buy that latte, king. Invest in yourself."

You're holding in laughter and the need to ask:

"Have you lost your mind? This is mental."

But instead, with the grace of someone who's fought in the trenches of team brainstorms before, you say:

"I'm having a hard time understanding your logic. Can you explain the thought process behind this?"

Liam lights up like a Christmas tree. "Absolutely! So the Gen Z demographic responds to emotional validation, right? Tom is that validation."

You nod slowly while mentally drafting your resignation letter and wondering if Tom can emotionally support you through this meeting.

What You Really Want To Say:

I can't do this fucking shit anymore. I'm drowning in work.

HR Approved Alternative:

I'm at full capacity on my existing projects right now. Would you like me to reprioritize instead?

Case File

You're trying to finish three decks, approve two invoices, and remember when you last consumed a vegetable. Just as you're about to shut your laptop and go cry in the shower, though, Jasmine from Ops strolls over holding a folder labeled "URGENT (but somehow not urgent until now)."

"Hey! Quick thing," she chirps, handing you what looks like 40 pages of spreadsheets and chaos. "Can you turn this around by EOD? Shouldn't take more than a few hours."

You stare at her like she's just asked you to rebuild the Eiffel Tower using Excel formulas.

You're close to breaking down and want to say:

"I can't do this f*%king shit anymore. I'm drowning in work."

But instead, through the hollow laugh of someone held together by caffeine and a broken Outlook calendar, you say:

"I'm at full capacity on my existing projects right now. Would you like me to reprioritize instead?"

Jasmine blinks.

"Oh! I didn't realize you were so busy!" She says, as she backs away like you're a wild raccoon who's had enough.

You nod, smile, and return to your screen, where the cursor blinks in silent judgment.

What You Really Want To Say:

Shut your trap before I lose my shit

HR Approved Alternative:

Let's park this for the time being

Case File

It's 9:00 a.m. You're in a Teams meeting and trying to stay positive, but Alice from Marketing won't shut up. She's now five minutes deep into a monologue about how the team needs a "QR code strategy that taps into the brand's higher purpose."

Nobody asked. Nobody even knows what she's saying. It's like corporate word soup, and somehow, she's quoting articles she half-read and interrupting every time someone else opens their mouth.

You try to jump in with something useful, but Alice steamrolls ahead, now pivoting into chakras and some article from Business Mindset Monthly (which might not even exist).

You're clenching your jaw so tight your molars start to hum.

You've got real deadlines, actual problems, and Alice's voice is now just corporate jazz in your ear canal.

You're on the verge of snapping:

"Shut your trap before I lose my shit, Alice!"

Instead, you channel every ounce of inner peace and say:

"Let's park this for the time being."

Which really just means: *If you say "brand alignment" one more time, I will combust in this swivel chair*.

Alice smiles proudly, thinking she's added real value. You mute your mic and seriously consider switching careers to a professional goat herder.

What You Really Want To Say:

I've had enough of your bullshit excuses

HR Approved Alternative:

I understand there have been some challenges, but let's focus on practical solutions that move the needle

Case File

It's a Thursday, and Kyle once again rolls into the meeting with the same energy as a deer caught in headlights. He's got that trademark line ready, like clockwork: "Yeah, I didn't get a chance to finish the deck because the Wi-Fi at my Airbnb in Tulum was super spotty."

You resist the urge to roll your eyes. This is the third week in a row Kyle's had an excuse that sounds like it was pulled from a Mad Libs: "I was locked out of my Google Drive." "My dog got into my charger cable." "Mercury's in retrograde."

Meanwhile, you and the rest of the team have been dragging this project uphill like it's the final challenge on *American Ninja Warrior: Corporate Edition*. Everyone's tired. Everyone's over it. Kyle, however, is still somehow one "tech issue" away from winning Employee of the Month — for least effort with most words.

You're tempted to say: "I've had enough of your bullshit excuses."

But you don't. What you actually say is:

"I understand there have been some challenges, but let's focus on practical solutions that move the needle."

Meaning? *Your laptop didn't fail you — your work ethic did. Let's get it together.*

Kyle nods solemnly, then immediately suggests pushing the deadline.

You smile through gritted teeth and quietly add "Tulum Wi-Fi" to the growing list of reasons you'll need therapy.

Thank you for reading this book!

I hope I got at least one laugh out of you :)

I would be incredibly grateful if you could take just 30 seconds to leave me a review! Reviews are crucial for an author's livelihood and surprisingly difficult to come by.

The more reviews my books receive, the more I can continue pursuing my love for creating books. If you have any thoughts about this book, please leave a review and let me know.

- Sam